Mama, I Heard Your Cry

MW01173331

Mama I Heard Your Cry

Mama, I Heard Your Cry

Mama, I Heard Your Cry

Scripture quotations, unless otherwise indicated, are taken from the *Holy Bible, King James Version*, Cambridge, 1769. Used by permission. All rights reserved.

The opinions expressed by the author are not necessarily those of Fountain of Life Publishers House.

Published by Fountain of Life Publishers House

P. O. Box 922612 Norcross, GA 30010
404-936-3989
Please Email Manuscripts to: publish@pariceparker.biz

Fountain of Life Publishing House is committed to excellence in the publishing industry. The Company reflects the philosophy established by the founder, based on Psalm 68:11, "The Lord gave the word and great was the company of those who published it."

Book design copyright © 2015 by Fountain of Life Publishers House. All rights reserved.
Cover Design by Parice Parker
Interior design by Phyllis R Brown
Editor: Phyllis R Brown

Published in the United States of America

ISBN: 978-0-9910627-3-7

TXU1-224-023

December 5, 2014

Mama 1 Heard Your Cry

Fountain of Life Publishers House

For book orders or wholesale distribution
Website: www.pariceparker.biz

Mama I Heard Your Cry

TABLE OF CONTENTS
I Wish

Chocolate Drop

Mama I Heard Your Cry

I Wish

*I wish I had a father that
showed me the way
A father that would have
taught me how to pray*

7

Mama 1 Heard Your Cry

INTRODUCTION

One afternoon, I sat down and thought about my life. I grew tired of the way my life had been going and I wanted nothing more, than for it to disappear. Many times, I have found myself wondering, why I was ever born? Why does God allow us to be born in this misery? My mind was boggled with so many events and people that have affected how and what I have become today. So, I pulled out a pen and a piece of paper and began writing about my life. As I sat there thinking, Mama was the first person that came to mind. I paused for a moment as tears flowed. I thought about the troubled times Mama had raising seven children, five girls and two boys. The whole time, Mama was trying to keep her eyes focused on the deliverance of God and instilling the same in us. I know that through her prayers, she kept hope alive.

Daily my mother endured persecution mentally or physically being abused by my father, who was a preacher of the gospel trying to save souls. The way I saw it, he preached the gospel on Sundays, while slowly killing my mother the rest of the week.

Mama went through so much and took a lot of things she didn't have to, in order to keep a roof over our heads and food in our bellies. She worked herself night and day to the bone, over-exhausting her body, just to raise her children. Mama tried so hard to keep the faith. So many times, I heard Mama cry, even though around us she tried to be strong turning her head to wipe a falling tear hoping we did not see her crying.

Now, that I have raised four girls practically alone, I feel her pain and the agony of her sorrows she had to bare. Although my life seemed to have been impossible to go any further, I now realize *that my mother's trials were much greater than my own. Only through the grace of God and the might of his mercy, I am able to tell someone about the struggles of my life.*

Many days and nights I saw my mother pray unto God. I believe she was praying for God to help her make it one more day as I have found myself doing quite often. I thank God for bringing me back to remembrance and pressing forth the effort of survival.

Today, because of my mother's tears and prayers. I am able to have the experience of being a mother of four beautiful girls that have brought me bundles of joy through seven precious grandchildren. As I sit here opening my life up to you, I have most definitely realized that my life is worth living. Turn the page, it will be well worth the time to read how my mother's tears and her prayers have saved my life.

Chocolate Drop

Mama I Heard Your Cry

I Wish

*I wish I had a father that
showed me the way
A father that taught me how to
pray*

Mama 1 Heard Your Cry

Chapter 1
Moving to Big Mama's House

Chapter 1

Moving to Big Mama's House

Reflecting back over the years in my life, I still remember many things as though it were yesterday. Sometimes when I reminisce, I smile and laugh because some memories were so funny; some, in particular, were joyful and some memories caused me to cry because they were so sad. Oftentimes, we wonder if there was just one thing that we could change, quite naturally I would. Many times my answer is yes, yes I wish I had just another chance to see my mother's beautiful smile; I wish many of days I was looking into her piercing light brown eyes. _Most of all to tell her just one more time how much I truly love her. If I had just one more tender loving moment with my mother to just give her a kiss and humongous hug, yes then I would. I really didn't begin to understand my father, until after his death. If we could only turn back the clock, and then would we? Yes, I would._

While thinking back through the years, the very first thing I remember is moving to Big Mama's house. I don't remember much, particularly, where we were moving from but I remember Big Mama's house. My oldest sister, Sasha, known for her teary eyes but extremely smart; I was next to the oldest. I always had to do all the cooking and work. Beatrice was always a jokester and bully in the family. One of my younger sister's Detra, she always picked on me and was bossy; last but not least. My baby sister Paula, she was always quiet and humble. I remember telling mommy how beautiful Big Mama's house was and mommy said, "I know baby, this is going to be our home." It had a white picket fence to go around the whole house, matching the color of the outside of the house. With all the colors of tropical flowers surrounding the front yard, look at all those colors, crimson red, fuchsia pink, sunburst gold, fully blossomed to true colors. All those beautiful flowers planted so neatly around the house; look mommy, every where we looked their was flowers. Mama, I can't believe this is going to be our new house.? It's so pretty, I love Big Mama's house. She was always so nice to us. As we continued to drive up in an old beat up station wagon, you can hear it about a mile away, I saw a little old lady sitting on the front porch. It was Big Mama and I said, "Mama, why do they call her Big Mama? She's the smallest lady I ever seen."

Mama, I Heard Your Cry .

Mama didn't, answer me. I guess she just didn't hear me. She was only about four feet tall and very petite in size, maybe to everybody else she looked big. We drove up to the front of the house so that the truck could fit in the driveway. Uncle Bill and daddy had all the large furniture pieces on the back of the pick-up truck and they were traveling behind us. Uncle Sammy drove up to the front of the house. The car was loaded with mostly boxes and clothes, such as our personal belongings. I smiled as I sucked on my red lollipop, then the closer we got I realized this is our first house. Then my lollipop juice begin to drip. It was strange to me, but in a good way as though I've always lived there. When Mama said, "we were moving." I didn't know that it wasn't going to be our own house, but I was still happy just to be living at Big Mama's house. As my Uncle Sammy drove up closer to the house, Mama said, "everyone *get out and help carry something in the house, Beatrice get back here and help, we have a lot to do before it gets too late." After we all got out of the car, I looked at all the stuff we had to help carry in the house, boy it seemed like we'll never get finished. I just wanted to run inside the house and finish eating my lollipop. It tasted so good and I wanted to go out to meet me some new friends. It was Mama (Pat Jones Crowder), my Father (Richard Wilbert Crowder), and my four sisters and I.*

Big Mama looked at all our stuff. I know she thought it was too much, but Big Mama never complained. I ran inside the house, then I looked and wondered how are all of us going to live here? It was only three bedrooms, one bathroom, a living room, and a kitchen for the eight of us to share. We really didn't care about being cramped up together because we just love Big Mama's house and this was our first house. I know Big Mama was thinking, she already raised mama from the age of eight years old, now I got to raise her children too? A mother's job is never done. I guess you can call it an eye for an eye and tooth for a tooth. Big Mama was getting older anyhow and she really needed some help around the house, then we needed a place to stay so I guess it worked out after all.

One thing I can surely say about Big Mama, she always kept a sparkling clean house, but this Saturday the air was extra fresh and clean with the windows up and the brisk air was blowing in up against the curtains. There in the midst of the light, I looked at Big Mama and thought how beautiful she was. Her smile was so glaring with deep dimples sinking in her jaws and very noticeable sparkling white teeth. She appeared to be so happy. I guess, she had been a little lonely without us. Her hair was silky jet black and very long only with just a few gray streaks at the time. She was part Cherokee Indian with smooth dark pecan baby skin and with a heart of gold glaring from the inside out. Everybody always said, t "I looked just like Big Mama." That is why they named me Matilia, after Big Mama's name. One time Big Mama noticed I was looking at her, she said, "This here is a sho nuf glorious beautiful day." Then mommy called, and I ran back outside to get some more stuff. This particular day the sky was crisp blue, but thank goodness it wasn't too hot because we had a lot of stuff to move into Big Mama's house. After about a few hours the moving was finished and we were able to go outside for a little bit while mommy cleaned up our stuff. "Y'all, before you go out and play make sure you get Paula her bottle so that she can stop crying," said mommy. The funniest thing is that Paula's bottle was an old Coca-Cola bottle. Mommy didn't have a real bottle. Then Big Mama said, "Let's go around to the corner store, Piedmont Super Market." That was Big Mama's favorite store because they used to always give her credit until she got paid. Back in those days, the store-owners of the neighborhood stores knew their customers very well and they gave Big Mama credit every week. As we walked back to the house with some groceries. I noticed that our house stood out like a white lily in a red bed of roses from all the other houses on the block. Big Mama's house was just stunning.

When we got back to the house, mommy seemed to have been getting so tired and breathless. She was even sweating and then

Mama, I Heard Your Cry

Big Mama told mommy, "Sit down and take a break. You can't do everything in one day." I know ma, I know. Matilia baby, I'm going to make you some fresh homemade chocolate chip cookies and I'm going to start on dinner. I know y'all are hungry. Yea, Big Mama that would be good. So Big Mama began the dinner. I was so happy because she can cook and we loved her cooking. I hope she's going to make her old-fashioned apple turn-overs and her homemade buttermilk biscuits that melt in your mouth. And, I'm so hungry my stomach has begun to growl. Detra's stomach had already started growling earlier. Come on y'all we have to get ready for our baths before dinner gets ready. So after dinner we can get in the bed, and Mommy said, "Find our church clothes for church tomorrow." After this day was over we all had a good night's rest due to all the moving and un-packing.

Mama, I Heard Your Cry

Early the next morning Big Mama had already started breakfast before we all woke up. It was another bright sun shinny day. Every Sunday, Big Mama wakes us up with good smelling breakfast and giving God praises even before we get to the church. One thing I can say is that Big Mama was a real Christian woman and so was mommy. Really, myself, I use to sometimes hate Sunday because we would have to go to church all day long. And when we use to get home sometimes it would be dark, late in the evening. My mother did not allow us to watch TV, go outside to play, or listen to the radio. She always said, "This is God's day and we are going to fully respect God on His day." My sisters and I were upset, almost every Sunday, because we knew that we could never get to go out and play with our friends. Big Mama and mommy would shout every Sunday in church. I never remember a

Sunday that they didn't shout and I know that they were shouting for real. I use to sit back and watch them praise God. One thing I learned not to do is play in church, talk in church, fall asleep in church or eat in church. If we did, either of these things we knew we would get a terrible whipping with a big long hickory stick and we automatically knew not to play in the Lord's house.

After church service later on in the evening, we all use to sit around the dinner table to eat because mommy and Big Mama had prepared dinner on Saturday nights. Sundays was a pretty big day for the both of them and they didn't believe in working, house cleaning or cooking on any given Sunday. Mommy began to serve dinner and boy was I hungry and ready to eat. This Sunday mommy was extra pretty, she also had long beautiful jet-black hair, light brown eyes, tan caramel skin tone, and a beautiful smile. Her face was long and slender; it was perfect without any makeup. When she looked at me I would always see the twinkle that resembled the diamond glitter in her eyes, her lips were astonishing naturally ruby red and when they were closed they formed a perfect heart shape. As her mouth opened to speak her teeth looked like a perfect set of pearls, very white and straight that peeked through her lips. As mommy continued to serve dinner I looked at her and thought to myself, I hope I grow up and be just as beautiful as my mommy. And then she sat down after serving dinner, we all bowed our heads and daddy blessed the food.

After we all ate dinner, Sasha and Beatrice had to clean off the kitchen table while mommy helped them to clean the kitchen, then daddy had to go somewhere.

He always said that, "he was going to church late on Sundays." I guess because he was a preacher too. Mommy didn't' even know he had already left until she called his name, Richard, and she didn't receive an answer. I told her he had already left and she appeared a little disappointed as usual. Nevertheless, mommy never said anything else about it. I tried to make mommy feel better so I told her that she and Big Mama were the best cooks in town and they had my vote, then mommy smiled. It was time for us to go to bed again so we bathed, brushed our teeth and said our prayers. After I got up off my knees, I ran into mommy's room to say good night and saw her kneeling and praying. So I tipped toed out, went back to bed and then I fell fast asleep.

I realized, Big Mama was more like a grandmother to us instead of a great aunt.

She never complained about us living there with her. I'm sure it wasn't easy at her age to live with crying babies. Big Mama had already raised my mother from the age of eight years old along with her own daughter, after her mother passed. Mama had two sisters and three brothers that were split up and lived with other family members.

It was a beautiful Saturday afternoon, the air smelled so fresh and clean. The wind was blowing and it felt so good when the cool breeze blew my way. The sky was blue as the ocean.

I was so proud of our new house, strangely, our house stood out like a white lily in a bed of red roses. I remember the grocery store across the street, Piedmont Super Market where Mama and Big Mama use to shop each week. Back in those days the store owners was really concerned and workers knew their neighborhood customers very well. Quite often he would give credit to us if we ran out of something we needed and Mama would pay him back.

Big Mama was a Christian woman just like my mother. She was such a beautiful person inside and out. She took good care of us like we were her own and she had a heart of gold.

We used to love Big Mama's cooking. Both of them really knew how to cook. They made homemade cookies that would melt in your mouth, old fashioned homemade apple turnovers, hot biscuits and oh! I can't forget the sweet potato pies. On Sundays, we always had a big dinner. Back in those days, people really knew how to cook, but Big Mama and Mama had my vote for the best cooks in town.

Mama, I Heard Your Cry

Almost a year had passed since moving in with Big Mama; it was time for me to start elementary school. I remember my first day. Mother walked me to school. I was so happy knowing how much she cared about me. By the time we got to the classroom, I don't know if I was more excited or scared. This was my first time in a classroom and to see all the beautiful arrangements on the walls was amazing. The alphabet, animals, and so much more. It was like visiting a museum.

The students were sitting at their desk quietly, everyone was staring at me and I was staring at them. I thought to myself, "So this is school?" My teacher's name was Mrs. Sim; she was an old woman. She looked to be about seventy years old. She was a short plump lady with such a friendly face. After Mama met Mrs. Sim, got me settled at my desk, she kissed me and said that she was going to work. Tears filled my eyes, I hated to see her go. Mrs. Sim was one of the sweetest and most understanding people you would ever want to meet. She had so much patience, and got along with everyone. Her personality was out of this world. Of all my teachers, and during all my years of school, I will always remember Mrs. Sim. I wanted her to teach me every year but I knew that was impossible. At the end of each day Sasha, my older sister, would come to my class to get me so that we could walk home together.

Mama cleaned houses for a living. She was employed by mostly Greeks but there were a few whites that she worked for. During this time she cooked, cleaned, ironed and whatever else that was needed for two families not including her own. When I was younger, many times I cried when Mama left to go to work. No one knew but me and God.

Mama, I Heard Your Cry

Mama use to walk to work because we didn't have a car. I would stand by the window with tears in my eyes watching her until she was out of sight. I did the same with Big Mama when she went to work. Their jobs weren't far from where we lived but it was a good long walk. I use to miss them so much and I wanted to be near them all the time.

Mama I Heard Your Cry

I Wish I Had

**A father that would tuck me in bed
A father that made sure my prayers were said**

Mama 1 Heard Your Cry

Chapter 2
A Preacher and a Painter

Chapter 2

A Preacher and A Painter

My daddy was a painter and a preacher. He was well known for doing such good work. He painted houses, apartment complexes, etc., he had more work than he could handle. Everyone loved his work. He was the best painter around.

He was a tall, slender, brown skinned man with only one eye. Daddy lost his eye cutting wood for the fireplace at the age of twelve. We did not get to spend a lot of time with my daddy because he was either at

33

work, in church or at an engagement of some kind. The only time we all spent time together was on Sundays, when we went to church together. He was a true Christian in my early years.

My daddy preached his first sermon at the age of twelve. Now that I think about it, I wonder if losing his eye had anything to do with him becoming a preacher. I never asked, if it was before or after? People that knew my daddy since he was a young boy use to talk about how good of a preacher he was. Family and friends from his hometown which was Chester, South Carolina would come to Charlotte just to hear him preach. My daddy was one of the best preachers I knew. Every time my daddy would pray or sing, tears would fill my eyes, not to mention the preaching, people would shout every time. I use to love hearing my father preach, he was one of the best.

Things were pretty good at this time. Each day when my daddy got home from a hard days work, he would ask us to clean the paint off his face. Paula would always cry because she wanted to help, but the ones that were old enough would take alcohol to clean his face. We use to battle over who would clean daddy's face. It was so much fun.

On Sunday's our parents made sure that we all went to church. Mama would dress us so beautiful every Sunday. She made sure that we wore white socks, black patent leather shoes and a white ribbon on our hair. On Sundays we would get to church about ten o'clock in the morning and most of the time we didn't get home until late Sunday evening. My daddy would have engagements at other churches to preach and Mama would always go to support him. We attended a Christian Baptist church of God. Sunday was a holy day. We weren't allowed to wash clothes, look at TV, or go out and play. This was the Sabbath day and Mama and Big Mama took it serious about keeping it holy. Big Mama didn't always go to the church we attended. She attended Mount Olive, a church that was down the street from our house. Sometimes I would walk with her to church if my daddy didn't have to preach.

Most Sundays we had other pastors over to join us for dinner. It was courteous and customary in our house for the children to wait for the pastors and other adults to eat before us. Many times I would look at them chomping on Mama's fried chicken, mashed potatoes, gravy, and collard greens, or whatever she cooked for Sunday and would *get angry. I wished they would hurry up and eat and quit talking so we could eat. One of us children would say, "Look at them, they have finished eating and are still sitting there." Another one would say that, "We were ready for them to get up from the table so that we children could eat."*

Mama and Big Mama would cook the Sunday dinners on Saturday nights, so that when we got home from church all they had to do was warm up the food. Everyone loved their cooking, especially during Christmas time. She would bake cookies, cakes and pies for the neighbors and, of course, most of the pastors that we knew.

I remember one Sunday Big Mama and Paula, my baby sister, rode home with Uncle Willie from church because Big Mama was getting too old to walk, like the rest of us.

Mama, I Heard Your Cry

Our church was a couple of miles away. Mama had warmed up Sunday's dinner and realized that Big Mama and Uncle Willie had not gotten there yet. At first she wasn't worried because Uncle Willie loved to talk so she figured they were still at the church or stopped by one of the members' homes. After about an hour, Mama began pacing the floor like she was trying to make a path from the kitchen to the living room. It was dusk dark before Big Mama, Uncle Willie and my baby sister Paula came home. They had been in an accident and Paula had broken her collar bone. Paula was all bandaged up around her neck and shoulders. She was a little baby about 6 months old. Mama started hollering because she didn't know what to think. We forgot to ask Big Mama if she was okay because we were all shocked at how Paula looked. Big Mama could not call Mama because we didn't have a phone. Poor thing, she didn't feel like walking from church, but her and Uncle Willie had to walk holding the baby from the hospital until a neighbor saw them and brought them the rest of the way home.

When I was about seven or eight years of age, things began to change so fast. Mama and daddy started arguing a lot and soon it became physical. It seemed like they could not get along anymore. At first daddy would push and shove or maybe slap Mama around a little bit. And in between the arguing and fighting my brother was born, Richard, Jr. I don't remember daddy ever hitting Mama while she was pregnant, but they would argue. The fighting resumed after Richard, Jr. was born, but more frequently and serious.

Mama, I Heard Your Cry

Big Mama would try to console us and keep us from crying, but she kept out of Mama and daddy's business as far as I know. She never said anything while we were around. About a year or so later my parents decided to separate and daddy moved out. That started another trend in our life with daddy leaving for a couple of weeks, then a month, and so on.

When we were older, during the summer, my daddy would take us to work with him to help him paint. During those times, my mother didn't have to work as hard and she would go and help him paint too. He would give all of us girls a small paint brush and he and Mama would have a regular sized one. We used the small brushes to paint the trimmings around the windows. We had so much fun helping daddy paint. He would buy us all a big lunch when we helped him. My sisters and I couldn't wait for lunchtime to eat. Eating out was a treat to us in those days and we enjoyed it every time. After eating all that food, we would be so full and didn't feel like getting back to work. But, we knew that we had to get the job done so we forced ourselves to paint again. I enjoyed working with my father during the summer. I often think of those good times. It was the only time I felt like he was a real father to us and that we were a real family.

Big Mama was getting older now and wasn't able to work any longer. Daddy had gone again and Mama couldn't afford to pay all the bills by herself. so they, decided to move in with Uncle Willie. We all went, except for my daddy. By this time my baby brother was born, Ben. Uncle Willie also had a three bedroom house with one bath, a living room and a kitchen. It was a little smaller and less *attractive than Big Mama's house but, the ten of us managed. Uncle Willie made us feel welcomed, however, Mama worked day and night to get a place of our own. It hurt me to see her work so hard.*

My mother hardly spent quality time with us, she worked all the time. Big Mama kept us while mother worked. We hardly saw Mama, she worked on Sundays and most holidays, cooking and cleaning for other people's families. She rarely had a day off. When she did take a day off she was sick. I wanted to enjoy her company sometimes when she was well, but whenever she had a day off sick or well. I was so happy just having her home with us. I remember the time I had a stomach ache like I had never had before. My mother needed the money so she needed to go to work; the only thing she knew to do was to pray. I know that my mother and God had a strong relationship, because before it was time for my mother to leave for work, my stomach ache was gone. God let her go to work in peace, knowing that I was alright.

Mama I Heard Your Cry

I Wish I Had

A father that would set me on his knee
And tell all the good things about me

Mama 1 Heard Your Cry

Chapter 3
Mother's New House

Chapter 3

Mother's New House

*M*onths had passed since we had seen or heard from my father. Mother finally saved up enough money to get us a place of our own. Uncle Willie hated to see us go, but understood that Mama wanted us to have more room and privacy. Mother thanked Uncle Willie for being so kind to us. Our house was a little bigger than before, and we didn't have a lot, but what counted most is that we had happiness. Of course, Mama was not going to leave Big Mama, she moved with us too.

The house had three bedrooms, one and a half baths, a living room, a small den, and a kitchen. It was enough room for the nine of us and we were thankful. The hardwood floors were shiny and we had an arch in the entrance of the kitchen from the living room. The outside didn't have any flowers growing; there were lots of trees in the back, including an apple tree. Mama was so proud of what she had accomplished. I prayed and thanked God for making my Mama so happy, and for giving her this house that she worked so hard to get.

Four Months had passed since we moved in our house. It was Saturday afternoon, we had just finished eating dinner and wasn't expecting company, but guess what? Father decided to pop up into our lives as though nothing ever happened. How did he find out where we lived? I thought to myself.

Mama, I Heard Your Cry

He was a smart man, he always found out what he wanted to know.

Mama and my sisters were sitting at the kitchen table talking and my brothers were outside playing. I was in the shower when the doorbell rang, mother answered the door. I heard a familiar voice and at that moment I didn't recognize who it was. Then I heard mother say, "Hi Richard, it's been a long time." She asked him, "What brought you back into our lives." I knew then that it was daddy. I hurried out of the shower, threw on my robe, and rushed into the kitchen. I gave him a big hug and said, "Daddy! I'm glad you decided to come home." All the time I was thinking to myself how much I hated him coming back. I knew he hadn't changed; I could see it in his face. I wondered how many times he was going to put us through this, especially my Mama. Coming in and out of our lives, knowing that he will never change.

Life was so peaceful when daddy was gone. I'm not sure how Mama felt about him. Now that I'm older, I know that she must have been lonely and loved him because she never dated anyone else while he was gone. Furthermore, she always had to work harder without daddy's income to help out.

Daddy had been drinking. I smelled loud aroma of alcohol on his breath when I hugged him. He was walking funny and his speech was a little slurred when he talked. This was the first time I had ever seen my daddy drunk. I could see the confusion and disappointment all in my mother's face. "Richard, you are drunk. Why did you come here this way?" Mama asked while shaking her head. "You are a minister, a leader for

Mama, I Heard Your Cry

God." My daddy flopped down on the couch. "Shut the hell up, I am a grown man and I can do what the hell I please." Mama burst into tears, "Richard, I can see you haven't changed, as a matter of fact you seem to have gotten worse." "You are not the Richard I use to know." Daddy yelled at Mama, "Bitch! Don't say nothing else, I don't want to hear this shit." I'm the man of this damn house, I thought you would be glad that I'm back."

My sisters and I were scared. Daddy was yelling at the top of his lungs and Mama was crying. The boys had gone back out to play, they were young anyway and didn't really know what was going on. We were sitting at the table hoping that daddy would not hit Mama again.

I whispered to Sasha, "I think he's gone crazy, who does he think he is?" I was so mad at daddy. We were having a quiet evening, enjoying each other. We didn't get that quality time with Mama often and he had to go and ruin it.

"Richard, you haven't called or wrote one letter and you expect to just walk back in here and be the man of this house that I worked so hard by myself to get?" my Mama yelled. Daddy slapped Mama across the face. "Oh bitch, you think you saditty now that you have your own place?" Mama touched the side of her face that daddy had just slapped, and went into the bedroom and tried to close the door. Daddy was right behind her and pushed the door open. "Don't you ever try to shut a door in my face you stupid bitch. Who do you think you are?"

That was daddy's favorite word to call Mama. I heard Mama whisper softly,

Mama, I Heard Your Cry

"Richard, do you have to call me dirty names in front of the children? I was only telling you what was right." Daddy said, "I already know right from wrong, I don't need you trying to tell me what to do." Daddy yelled as he lifted his hands to hit Mama again.

I yelled, "Leave her alone." "I wish you would disappear out of our lives forever." Daddy slapped me on the right side of my face as hard as he could. It happened so fast, it scared me and it stung so bad that I couldn't help but to cry. I felt the side of my face, I thought that part of it was gone.

Mama rushed to my side. "Get out Richard, don't you ever hit her like that again, get out!" He ignored her and said, "Fuck you." "I'm going out for another drink, I hope that you will be sleep when I get back, arguing all the time is getting on my nerves."

Mama, I Heard Your Cry

Mama yelled, "Richard! You don't need another drink, it will only make matters worse." Mama turned around and started toward the kitchen with tears in her eyes. "I've tried so hard to be the perfect wife, said mother, sometimes I feel like giving up." I said to Mama, "Do what makes you happy, it's your life."

Mama went back to her room, I could hear her crying. I wanted to go comfort her, but I knew she wanted to be alone. I went to check on mother before going to bed. As I entered the room, I saw Mama sitting at the foot of the bed, I asked her was she alright? She said, "Yea sweetheart, I'm fine." I kissed her good-night and went to bed.

The next morning when I got up, Mama was still asleep. I didn't wake her because she needed to get her rest. Suddenly, I heard the turning of the key in the door. I knew that it was daddy. My heart started beating fast, I felt trouble. This time he was drunker than before, stumbling over everything, soon he fell to the floor. The noise woke Mama up. Mama rushed to the living room to see what had happened. Daddy was lying on the floor knocked out. Mama left him lying there. She told us not to wake him, let him sleep it off.

Finally, he woke up and came to his senses for a moment. Mama didn't say a word, she went in the kitchen and started preparing breakfast as usual. She fixed daddy a cup of coffee. After we finished eating, daddy was sitting at the table looking pitiful and looking ashamed. He apologized promising that it wouldn't happen again.

The following week-end it happened again and again. Nothing changed, matters got worse each time. One lie after another. Promises! Promises! The only thing was I never got use to it. Daddy kept Mama upset. He was controlling in every way. Mama had to really have loved daddy to put up with the agony and pain for so many years. I was tired of daddy putting Mama through pure hell, but Mama accepted him back in her life each time.

Father's drinking problem did not stop. He came home drunk practically every week-end. As soon as he came in the door, he started arguing about something. One night he came home drunk, we were in bed; all of us girls were still awake when he came in. He asked Mama, what did she cook? Mama answered, "Richard, I didn't cook today. I wasn't feeling well, we ate sandwiches. If you are hungry, I will cook you something in a minute. "Daddy raised his voice, "I want to eat now! Not tomorrow! Not next week, but now!" He was yelling at the top of his voice as loud as he could. Mama said, "Richard, people are asleep in this house, do you have to talk so loud. I'm getting ready to cook now, getting out of bed." All hell broke loose. I heard a slap, then something falling. I knew that daddy was fighting Mama again. I heard Mama say, "Richard, don't hit me again."

I was lying across the bed. We jumped out of bed and ran to the kitchen to see what was going on. I couldn't believe what my eyes saw. Daddy was beating Mama with both fists like she was a strange man who stole something from him. It was like a bad dream seeing my Mama getting knocked around like she was nothing. She was yelling for him to stop. Daddy picked up a chair from the kitchen table and hit her with it with no mercy. Mama put both arms up to her face

Mama, I Heard Your Cry

trying to protect herself. My sisters and I were trying to hold daddy's hands, but he was moving too fast. We tried to help mother, but we had little luck. Daddy shoved Detra away and she fell to the floor and hit her head on the couch. My two youngest brothers were sleeping away. Daddy kept beating Mama and we were screaming, begging him to stop. Sasha grabbed a knife from the drawer and yelled, "Daddy, if you hit Mama one more time, I will kill you!" I believe she meant every word and daddy did too because he stopped beating Mama, turned around, snared at Sasha, picked up his coat and stormed out of the door.

I was so glad he left. My sisters and I went over to pick Mama up off the floor. Big Mama tried to help but we handled it. As we grabbed for Mama's arm, she screamed. I asked her, "What was wrong"? She cried, "I can hardly move my arm, be careful, it hurts." I knew then that her arm was broken. I hated daddy for abusing Mama the way he did. I wanted to kill him at that moment. That night I prayed to God that he never return. We decided to take mother to the hospital to get checked. When we arrived they took her back immediately to examine her. My sisters and I waited in the waiting room. Big Mama kept my two brothers while we were at the hospital. Soon the doctor and Mama came out together, he explained to us that Mama's arm was broken in two places and that she was to take it easy for a few days. When I got home, I wanted to curse my daddy for everything he was worth. I was so angry at him. I didn't speak to him for a week. My father made it a habit of beating my mother constantly. He thought nothing of it, it was like drinking a bottle of liquor. It was a regular routine for him. Many nights I heard Mama begging daddy to stop beating her. We heard her cry many times and couldn't do anything to help her.

I remember times when daddy would come home intoxicated, the least little thing we did he would start beating on us. Most times he would go from one to the other beating us. We didn't have to do anything. Half the time he would beat us for no reason. He called us bitches, whores, prostitutes, any name he thought of - that's what we were. He abused, mistreated, and misused us.

I will never forget the time daddy took off his belt and threatened to beat us because the dishes weren't washed. It was only a few dishes in the sink, he didn't ask any questions, he just started beating us with the belt. He beat us until blood ran from our skin. He used all his strength and every muscle in his body when he hit us with the belt. I use to ask God, why was I ever born? Another time he was angry with my older brother Richard, because he didn't finish his homework. Daddy took both hands hitting my brother over his ears. He would do this often to all of us. He would use both hands at the same time, sometimes my hearing would go away for a few seconds. I often wondered is this the reason my older brother Richard can't hear well today. He is nearly deaf. We have to yell loud for him to hear us. The doctor said that the majority of his ear drums were gone, and that there was a fifty-fifty chance that an operation would not help his hearing loss, and that he probably would lose all of his hearing.

Father was very mean to us, he showed no love, no concern, and no attention. I use to think he had no heart, perhaps no soul. I

Mama, I Heard Your Cry

cannot remember one time that my daddy ever told me that he loved me. Not one time has he taken me to the circus, tucked me in bed, or read me a bed-time story. I cannot remember one time that I ever sat on his knee and had the chance to tell him how I really felt inside. Many times I wanted to tell my father what I thought of him. I kept it to myself. I went that extra mile for Mama. Now that things were better, and Mama was well again, daddy thought that it was best if he left. I was so happy to hear the good news. It was a big relief for everyone. Everything was back to normal. With everything happening the way it did, and Mama having gone through so much, the years were flying by.

Three years had gone by, we heard nothing from father. Mama seemed worried the whole time he was gone. I knew that she still loved him with all her heart.

Mama I Heard Your Cry

I Wish I Had

**A father I could have faith in
A father that I wouldn't be
ashamed to take around my
friends**

Mama 1 Heard Your Cry

Chapter 4
From High School to Barber School

Chapter 4

From High School to Barber School

I was in high school already, enjoying being a cheerleader, rooting for every game our school was playing against. I met new friends, and occasionally, we would go out on dates with some of the guys on the team. My friend, Sandy, would come over my house each day after school, and we would study together. During the week days while school was going on, I couldn't go visit my friends, only on the week-ends and when there was a game at school. I was able to attend because I was part of it. My high school years were great. I could function and concentrate on my work better since daddy was gone out of our lives.

I remember the day my oldest sister graduated. It was a big day for us, we all were very excited and anxious to have such a talented person to speak at our school (Second Ward Junior High). The speaker was Martin Luther King, Jr. He came to speak in 1963. I will always remember that year. I graduated the next year, during 1964. The day of my graduation. Mama looked at me and smiled, she whispered, "I'm proud of you." I felt good knowing that I had made it this far. Six months had passed since graduation. Mama insisted that I go to college. I wasn't too excited about going to college just yet. I wanted to release myself of the pressure I tackled with while in high school. I needed a break. Mama didn't realize what I was going through at the time. To keep her happy, I agreed to go to college. Mother wanted us to get an education, so that we wouldn't have to work as hard as she did in this life. I didn't want to go four years of college like my older sister, Sasha. At the time, she was attending Hampton Institute in Virginia. So the next day, I talked it over with my friend Sandy; she suggested that I go to Barber College. She said, "it only took nine months to finish."

When Mama got home from work that evening, I explained it to her. She thought that was a good idea. The next day, Mama called Uncle Fred, who was my father's brother, who lived in Winston-Salem, North Carolina a very beautiful place. Mama wanted me close to a family member since this was my first time living away from home.

Mama, I Heard Your Cry

When I got home the next afternoon, Mama said, "Guess what?" I said to her, "don't tell me that my long lost daddy found his way back home, Mama laughed, and said no silly, "I thought to myself, thank God." She said, that "Uncle Fred had called and said that there was a Barber school in Winston-Salem." I said, "thank you Lord!" When are we leaving? Mama said, "that we will be leaving Monday." Uncle Fred will be down to pick us up. I was ready for a new start. I ran in the room to pack. I paused for a moment, I thought about Big Mama, who would take care of her while I'm gone? Since mother had to work, my older sister was already in college. But Big Mama did most things on her own. Plus, I knew that mother would take good care of her.

Monday finally arrived, Uncle Fred was on time. When he walked in the house, he asked, me was I ready for the trip? I said, "yes, of course." I've been waiting all weekend, let's travel. I rushed and called my friend Sandy, and told her that "I was on my way to Barber school and that I will keep in contact with her." Uncle Fred smiled and helped put the luggage in the car, we were on our way.

We arrived in Winston-Salem in an hour. Uncle Fred took us directly to the school. We got there a few minutes before it opened. We sat in the car eating snacks and enjoying each other's company while waiting for someone to come and let us in. Finally, Mr. Richard Thomas arrived, who was one of the instructors that taught at the school; we introduced ourselves, and he began touring us around the school, explaining the prices of everything. Mother told Mr. Thomas that I would be starting school Tuesday, and that she would send the tuition with me to pay for my class. Just before leaving Mother and Uncle Fred shook hands with Mr. Thomas, and said it was a pleasure meeting him, then we left.

When we left the school we went straight to Uncle Fred's house. As we entered the door I smelled a variety of food, Aunt Joyce had cooked up a storm. Aunt Joyce and my cousins were sitting in the den waiting on us. We were so excited to see each other because we hadn't seen each other since we were small. Everyone was laughing and talking. I was so hungry I could almost taste the food. I tried to cut the conversation short, but they kept talking. Finally, we ate. After dinner I went to bed. I was tired and sleepy. Mama, Aunt Joyce and Uncle Fred sat in the den laughing and talking about the good old days. The next morning after breakfast Uncle

Mama, I Heard Your Cry

Fred took Mama to the station to catch her bus. Mama kissed me good-bye and said that she would call us when she got home. The next morning, Aunt Joyce took me to Barber school. That evening, Uncle Fred and my cousin Penny, who was Uncle Fred's daughter, came to pick me up from school. We didn't go directly home, we drove around for a while sight-seeing, and stopping here and there, just having fun. Our last stop was Dairy Queen, Uncle Fred got us some ice cream and we went home. I enjoyed riding with Penny and Uncle Fred, he was my favorite uncle. Aunt Joyce and Uncle Fred treated me like one of their own. He was more than a father to me. I really miss Aunt Joyce and Uncle Fred. After I finished barber school, I lived in Winston-Salem for a year. When I received my barber's license to cut hair, I decided to go back home to Charlotte, North Carolina, and get a job there. When I got home, I started getting sick off and on, after a few weeks I decided to go to the doctor and get a checkup. Guess what? I was pregnant. This would be my first child, I was so disappointed and upset. Joe was still in Winston-Salem. He wasn't coming home until the next month. He had one more month to finish school and I didn't want to ruin it. After he had finished school and got home, I waited until the next day to talk with him about my situation. Joe was one of my classmates that I met in barber school. We became good friends, and fell in love. The next day I talked with Joe, he was more excited than I was, I was shocked. I didn't know what to think. After we had talked about it, I asked Joe to meet me at my mother's house to break the news to her. I was afraid because I didn't know how Mama would react. The next day Joe came over, Mama wasn't home yet, after waiting for a while, Mama soon came home. At first Joe was pacing the floor in the same spots, back and forth back and forth, he was acting like he was the one pregnant. Mama noticed him pacing the floor and asked him if anything was wrong? He said, "yes Mrs. Crowder, don't get alarmed, it's nothing bad." That's when Joe let it all out. Mama said with a trembling voice, "What? How did it happen?" She said, before thinking. I was scared and ashamed. During my pregnancy Mama treated me like I was the only child. She waited on me hand and foot. This was the kind of mother I had. She was forever comforting me.

Mama I Heard Your Cry

I Wish I Had

A father that showed me more love
A father to let me know I was often thought of

Mama 1 Heard Your Cry

Chapter 5
Big Mama Left Us

Chapter 5

Big Mama Left Us

My first child was born March 16, 1967. She put the sparkle back in my eye when I first saw her, Deona Crowder. Joe and I dated a few more months before he decided to join the Army. It was absurd to ever let him join the Army. I couldn't talk him out of it, he had made up his mind. I knew then, that the relationship wasn't going to last. I thought about it a few days and told Joe that it was best if we went our separate ways because it wouldn't work out for us. I would rather him to be here with

me and the baby, but he chose otherwise.
Today we are best friends.

The next week, I was coming home from
visiting a friend, me and the baby. I noticed a
lot of cars were in the yard. I didn't know
what to think. I jumped out of the cab without
paying, and ran into the house. I asked,
"Mama what had happened?" She said, "We
don't know." This morning after you left, Big
Mama complained about her head hurting
bad. After a while, she said, "that it was
hurting worse than before." I gave her some
medicine thinking that it would make her feel
better but, she got even worse. We rushed her
to the hospital, and before they admitted her,
she had passed. They couldn't detect what
caused her death. I called her daughter,
Paula, already. The aunt my baby sister was
named after. She is on her way down from
Washington, D.C. The doctor just called and

asked us to come to the hospital. I'm so sorry sweetheart. Immediately, I burst into tears, I couldn't believe that Big Mama was gone. And what hurt most, I didn't get to say good-bye. I will always remember Big Mama as long as I live. She was the only aunt that we really knew. Everything seemed to happen to the good people, nothing happened to the bad - this is my motto. Big Mama died on July 20, 1967. I knew that Mama was sad, she and Big Mama were very close. Actually, Big Mama was like a mother to mama pretty much all she knew. Big Mama would always come to mother rescue, I know mama is going to really miss Big Mama. Especially, with mothers mama dying when she was so young. Mother continued working daily trying to keep all the bills paid. She was persistent.

Mama, I Heard Your Cry

A few months had passed since I heard from Joe. It was time for me to go to work. I needed a fresh start. The following week I started working at Johnson's barber Shop, a few blocks from our house. It was in walking distance. Mr. Johnson was the owner. He was a tall slim brown skinned man who wore glasses. Mr. Johnson hired me the same day I applied for the job. It was a shock to me that he let me work on the same day I applied. When I got home late that evening, Mama asked where I'd been. I told her that I had been working. She said, "Really, where?" I was so excited. I answered her and said, "A few blocks up the street, it's within walking distance. Johnson's Barber Shop." Did he really hire you that fast? I said, "Yes Mama."

Mama had to quit one of her jobs to help me out with the baby. Mama loved her grandchildren. I wasn't the only one that had a child, my other sisters had children too, but this was my first baby. I had only been on the job a couple of days, the third day when I went to work, I noticed this man looking in from the window, he was just staring at me while I was cutting hair; I was getting nervous. At first I thought he was looking for someone. I didn't know what he wanted. I asked Mr. Johnson did he know the guy looking in the window. He said yes, that's Steve. He hangs around here a lot. He's a good guy. He's never seen a woman working here before. I asked, "Does he work?" Mr. Johnson said, "he is a brick mason, you know how that goes, you work when you want to work, or when someone has a job for you to do." I said, "Oh!" I understand now. Soon Steve walked in, he sat down and started reading the paper. Every time I look at him he was staring at me. I said to myself, "I wish that he would quit staring at me, he's making me nervous." At that moment, he asked Mr. Johnson, "Who is the new barber?" He said, "Matilia, she's only been here a few days." He asked Steve if he would like her to cut his hair. She's a good barber. He said, "Sure, I'll give her a try." He sat down in the chair, and said fix me up. I might have a hot date tonight. I said, I'll do my best. We both smiled, and I started cutting his hair. When I finished he looked at me and winked his eye whispering, one day you are going to be my wife. I looked at him with a smile on my face, and said, "you know more than I do." As he was walking toward the door, I yelled, "Wait a minute!" I forgot to give you one of my business cards. As I handed the card to him, he said to me, "I'll see you next week." The next week when he came to the barber shop he asked me out to dinner. I accepted the invitation. When I had finished my work for the evening, he picked me up and we had *dinner, then we went to the movies. We had so much fun going to dinner, movies, and on picnics. I really thought that he was the right man for me this time. We dated at least a year, then we got married.*

Mama 1 Heard Your Cry

I Wish I Had

**A father that taught me right
from wrong
A father that I would be happy
to see come home**

Mama I Heard Your Cry

Chapter 6
My Marriage

Chapter 6

My Marriage

We had a big wedding in his home town, a lot of people showed up Great Falls, South Carolina. My mother didn't approve of the wedding, but I married him anyway. The day of our wedding Steve had all the guests waiting, and he was nowhere to be found. His next door neighbor, Ruth, suggested that we go look for him at the golf course, she said that was his favorite spot. He was addicted to golfing. Mother begged me to cancel the wedding, but I was too embarrassed to. Him being late was already embarrassing enough to have to go _look for him on my wedding day. When we got to the golf course, there he was. I walked across the field to get Steve. He said he wasn't going anywhere until he shot five more holes, and he didn't until he finished playing the game. I should have canceled the wedding, mother knows best. Love can make you do foolish things sometimes. Steve's mother owned the house in Great Falls, South Carolina. We had spent two weeks there before we got married. About a couple of months after I had gotten married, I found out that I was pregnant with my second child (Pat Culp). She was born June 13, 1970. When Steve found out that I was pregnant, he left and went back home to his mother, who lived in Winston-Salem, NC. He was never a responsible man to take care of his family. He depended on his mother most of the time. His mother had already moved to Winston-Salem when I met Steve. We used her house_ *for special occasions, because the rest of her children were on their own. Today Steve is living in the house in Great Falls, SC. As long as I have been knowing him he's never had a place of his own. He has always lived with his mother and my mother most of the time. He use to get away with his good looks. My husband reminded me of my father in a lot of ways. He ran in and out of our lives, just like my father did. I am so glad that I had a good mother that really supported me in my time of need. One afternoon when Mama got home from work, she had started preparing dinner. I noticed all of a sudden it got quiet in the kitchen. I went to see why it was so quiet, Mama was leaning over the stove, like she was going to pass out in a moment. I asked her, "what was wrong?" She said, Matilia Mae darling, I'm hurting in the lower part of my stomach. I don't know why it started hurting. I haven't lifted anything heavy. It's* been hurting practically all day. I've never hurt like this before. I said, "Mama may be you need to lie down and rest a while," but she insisted on cooking anyway. The next day she went to work as usual. When she got home that evening she complained again about her stomach, it was worse this time. I advised her to make an appointment to see the doctor to check her and see what could be wrong. She was lucky, the same afternoon she called, she was able to make an appointment for the following day. She got up early that next morning, poor Mama was trying to get dressed by herself. I finished helping her get dressed so that she would be on time. Mama had gotten up real early. I asked her, "Why are you up so early?" Mama said, "she couldn't sleep." She tossed and turned all night, she kissed me and left going to the doctor.

Mama I Heard Your Cry

I Wish I Had

A father that would wear a smile
A father that who remembers that I am his child

Mama I Heard Your Cry

Chapter 7
Mama Pain & Suffering

Chapter 7

Mama Pain & Suffering

*T*me had passed quickly. I was getting worried, I haven't heard from Mama since she left. I waited a few more minutes before I got too excited. I then called the doctor's office, I got no answer. Evidently they were closed. I thought to myself, "Where is she?" "What could have happened?" I waited a few more minutes to see if she would call, but the phone never rang once. My last resort was to check with the hospitals. First I called Charlotte Memorial, no Pat Jones*

Mama, I Heard Your Cry

Crowder, secondly I called Presbyterian Hospital, she hadn't been admitted there; last I called Mercy Hospital and she was admitted there. I asked the nurse how long had she been there. The nurse said, "about three hours or more." I got dressed quickly and rushed over to the hospital. When I got there, Mama had tubes everywhere and an IV in her arm. I asked the nurse why she was hooked up to all these tubes. She wasn't that sick when she left home this morning, what happened? The nurse answered, "Your mother is a sick woman, we have examined her, taken x-rays, and run some tests; the tests show that she has cancer of the intestines." We won't know all the details until we operate. She said, that "she was sorry." I burst into tears, the thought of losing my mother was too much to bare. I couldn't understand why this had to happen to her. The tears continued to run down my cheeks. I couldn't help but to cry seeing Mama lying there helpless. I thought to myself, "She worked hard all her life just to die." Life is unpredictable. The nurse told us that she might have to have surgery; first they were going to run some more tests. She looked at me and smiled and said, "we will do all we can to save your mother." I was so worried about Mama, it was like a dream. I didn't want to believe it. I went to the window and looked up at the sky, and asked God why? Why Mama? It was such a beautiful day in June and my poor Mama was lying in the hospital with cancer. My mother had worked all her life, she never went to the beach, she never had a vacation, and all she did was worked for as long as I can remember. She never had a life. I wish we could live this life all over again, maybe things could have been different, but we only live once.

Mama, I Heard Your Cry

We never got to go to the circus, the zoo or Disney World, but I thank God for having a mother that loved us, she showed it in every way.

After so many days of suffering, the doctor sent Mama home until time for the surgery. There was nothing else that they could do until they ran more tests to really be sure about everything. The doctor gave her a shot for her pain, and wrote her a prescription for pain medicine. He said, "we could take her home until further notice." I felt so sorry for Mama. I remember the times she was taking care of us, now we were taking care of her. I didn't mind, because she did everything for us. I wanted to do something special for her when she got home. I cooked her a special meal that day, not realizing that it would be her last. I cooked collard greens, yams, fried chicken, I made potato salad, corn bread, hot biscuits, and tea to drink. I tried to cook her favorites. That particular day Mama didn't want me to serve her in bed, she wanted to eat at the table with the rest of us. After dinner Mama went to her room to lie down. Later that night while getting ready for bed, I heard a noise, so I went to check on Mama. As I approached her room, I heard Mama praying; asking God to ease her pain and let her go to sleep in peace. I knew that she was hurting. I could hear the trembling in her voice. She was praying like it would be her last prayer. I couldn't stand to see her suffer anymore.

My Mama always truly was a praying woman. Today I'm living because of her prayers. As I walked over to the window, I looked toward the sky a second time; it was so pretty and blue. I just wished that my Mama's life was half the color of the sky. As I was looking up, I asked God, what did Mama do to deserve this? She was a good mother and a good wife. I never understood why all the good people seem to do most of the suffering.

Three weeks had passed and Mama was still in pain suffering daily. It hurt me to see Mama suffer, but there was nothing I could do but pray. When I went back to the room Mama asked me to pray for her, this was Mama's first time ever asking me to pray for her. I was surprised that she asked, but it was no sin to pray, she would always pray for us. Softly I whispered a prayer for her pain to go away and that she would be able to rest in peace every night.

One morning I was awakened out of my sleep hearing Mama praying again, and moaning. I asked God, what could I do to help *ease her pain, a voice spoke to me at that moment and told me to get out of bed and go lay hands on Mama and pray with all my heart, and she would be healed. I just couldn't, I never knew why. Until this day, I regret that I did not obey God. I knew that it was him, he only tells you good things. Often it comes to mind, if only I had obeyed, would things have been different? Would Mama have been healed? Most of all, would she have been alive today?*

I couldn't stand to see mother suffer any longer so I got mother dressed and took her back to the hospital. When we arrived they admitted her immediately. After they placed her in a room, I left because I knew that she would be alright. Later, the doctor called and told us that they had taken her into surgery to find out what was really the problem. We were all very nervous and afraid.

Mama, I Heard Your Cry

The next day when the phone rang I was afraid to answer. It was the nurse and she asked, "Is this the Crowder's residence?" I said, "Yes, this is the Crowder's residence" with a tremble in my voice. My heart was beating so fast, she wanted us to come to the hospital immediately. My sisters, brothers, and I rushed over to the hospital. When we arrived Mama was out of surgery. We had to wait for her to fully recover. We were all waiting in the waiting room, after an hour or so we thought it was best if we called our father and let him know what was going on. When we finally reached our father, we explained to him Mama's situation. It took father two hours before he got to Charlotte. Mother and father were separated at the time, and father had moved to Winston-Salem with his brother, Uncle Fred. When father got to the hospital we were waiting in the waiting room. Finally, the doctor came *out, he had a sad look on his face. I thought Mama had passed already. I jumped up and said, "She's still alive, isn't she?" The doctor answered, "sure, she's alive." He said, "I want to have a talk with the family," before he could get the words out my husband walked in. I asked him how he knew about mother, he said that "father had mentioned it to him." The doctor started telling us her condition. He said to my father, "your wife was a strong woman." She has worked herself to death, "there's no strength in her body for her to go any further." We discovered that the cancer had eaten up the majority of her intestines, it had spread; that's why her stomach was in so much pain. The reason why we called everyone to the hospital is that she was losing so much blood. We thought we were going to lose her. The doctor said, "I don't think that she will last much longer." I often wondered what her purpose was here on earth. She* went through so much for nothing. After a long wait they finally brought Mama to her room. She was still asleep. All we could do was sit by her bedside and empathize with her. We all were still waiting for her to awake. Finally, she opened her eyes, a peculiar thing happened, she looked at us one by one from head to toe. I knew then that I was losing my mother. She remembered everyone. She said, "I'm leaving you now." I said to her, "Mama don't say that, you will be around a long time." She said no, "let me finish baby, I don't have much time. I want you all to know that I love all of you, no matter what. I want you to always stick by one another regardless. Promise me that you will do this, we all made that promise to her, and we have kept that promise." We were all standing by her bed side. She looked up at father and said, "I know that life wasn't what we expected, but look what we got out of it, seven beautiful children." Father said to mother, "it was our life." Her last words, she asked my sisters to, "take care of me and my baby brother Ben." Only she and God knew the reason. She then closed her eyes as though she was going to sleep. My sister, Beatrice, started screaming to the top of her voice, the nurse took her out of the room so that she wouldn't disturb the other patients. Poor Sasha fell to her knees begging God to spare Mama's life. I heard her saying over and over, please God, please God! It was too late she was already gone. I was like a lost sheep in the wilderness. I shook Mama, I called her name, she never opened her eyes, and she never answered. I fell to my knees asking God to bring her back just for a little while, the nurse came in the room and helped me off the floor. She put her arms around me trying to comfort me. She said to me, "I know that you will miss your mother, but God knows the best for us all." At least she won't have to suffer anymore. She is in a better place where there is no more pain. I couldn't keep the tears from coming. This was my first time experiencing losing someone so close to me, less known my mother. One thing Mama did experience in life, something she always wanted to do was ride a plane. My sisters, brothers and I made that possible. She went to visit my daddy once in Bermuda, she talked about it often, how much she enjoyed the trip. Nevertheless, she visit him in Bermuda when he was also with another woman. She loved my daddy so much and she was faithful until the end. No matter what, he was her husband. And, the thought of the plane ride made her happy from then on out she always wanted to ride a plane again. But, I am grateful we was able to make her first plane ride possible.

Mama, I Heard Your Cry

My mother was my world, there is not a day that goes by that I don't think of her and Big Mama. She just didn't live long enough. She died at an early age, she was only fifty - two years old. She died on my second oldest daughter's birthday, Yvonne Culp, June 13, 1972.

I know that God has a plan for all of us, no one really know what our plans are. I understand that I can't live forever, and I can't tear down what God has built up. We live this life and we die when it's over. This is why we should live it to the fullest, and make the best of it. I miss my mother so much. All the money in the world couldn't have taken the place of my mother. I thanked God every day for the mother I had.

After the death of my mother, my life was so sad. I just couldn't get over her death

Mama, I Heard Your Cry

I was still living in the same house, imaging her walking around, and imaging hearing her voice. I missed all of that. She and I lived together so long I couldn't get use to living without her. My husband was home with me, but it still felt like I was all alone. Without my mother it was miserable for a long time. I thank God for helping me to see the good side of life, and for being a mother for me so many times. Without faith and His help, I couldn't have made it this far. Three years had passed since the death of my mother. My husband, Steve, was still running in and out of our lives. During this time, my third child was born, Marice Culp. She was born November 24, 1973. Things were not getting any better for Steve and me. He would come down, get me pregnant and he was gone again. I was so naive I would always let him come back into my life. The last time Steve and I were together I got pregnant again with my last child, Pat Culp, who was named after my mother. She was born December 29, 1974. I regret that my mother didn't get to see my two youngest daughters. I know that she would have loved them to death like the rest of her grandchildren.

Mama I Heard Your Cry

I Wish I Had

A father I could have gone to
for advice
A father that had greater
respect and love for his wife

Mama 1 Heard Your Cry

Chapter 8
Broken Promises

Chapter 8

Broken Promises

My husband made so many promises and never fulfilled any of them. I let him move back in with me for the fourth time trying to make the marriage work, after so many years. He promised to get a job. He was a brick mason but, didn't like working. I was having it hard trying to raise four daughters as a single parent, and trying to keep the house. I didn't want to lose what Mama had worked so hard for. My husband enjoyed himself riding up and down the road for pleasure. The gas was already off at the house. I couldn't afford to keep up the mortgage payment and the utilities. I had a choice, so I did my best paying for the mortgage. I had to have somewhere for my children and I to live.

I used to feel so sorry for my oldest daughter, Deona. She had to get dressed in the cold. We had the oven on but, it was still cold. We had a big house. We had no food. I didn't know what we were going to do from one day to the other because times was so hard for me. I took one day at a time and prayed for God to make the way. I use to give my daughter a slice of bread for breakfast each morning and a glass of water. When she came home we ate whatever we had around the house. Very few mornings she ate a decent or hot breakfast. We stayed alive thank God. No one knew what I was going through. It had to be a God for us to have survived and moments like these I miss mom more. The next morning I noticed that the fireplace was burning. Oh, what a warm relief. I thought that Steve had borrowed money from someone that he knew. I ignored it and didn't ask any questions. I was glad that we had heat because it had been really cold. Later, that afternoon I started outside to get the clothes off the line. As I opened the door, I suddenly realized there were no steps. I said to myself, "Where in the hell is the steps? They were here yesterday!" I asked Steve about the steps, he said that, "he had cut the steps up for wood to go in the fireplace." At that moment he made me lose my religion. I said some horrible things and before I knew it, I said, "You lazy bastard, you could have walked around outside and found wood for the fireplace. Suppose one of the children had gone out the back door. It would have been a disaster; you wouldn't have given a damn!" I was so mad at Steve for putting our life in jeopardy. I almost stepped out the door, not realizing that there were no steps. I thank God that he saved me. I told Steve to pack his clothes and be on the next bus to Winston-Salem. I can do bad by myself. I sent him home to his mother. We had no gas, no food, my poor baby was dressing in the cold, now we have no steps. I didn't need Steve. He didn't make any effort to help me or support his children. I felt much better now that I was living alone. It was less pressure on me and less I had to worry about. I didn't realize it, but I was alone all the time. My husband was a sorry man. He thought his good looks, pretty brown eyes, fine curly hair, and his light caramel skin was going to continue giving him free ride through life. Anybody that will cut wood from their house they are still living in, especially their steps, how are you going to get in and out of the house? Use a ladder? They have got to be mentally ill, crazy or sorry as hell! Our steps were very high. I would have killed myself if I had stepped down. God saved me.

Life must go on. I hadn't heard from my husband since he left. Three months had passed. I had already decided to go on with my life. After the death of my mother, I couldn't take any more life surprises or heartaches.

Many times my children and I use to be so hungry, nobody knew but God and me. During these times I would think of my mother. I remember the time I only had four slices of bread, four pieces of bologna and one small can of chicken noodle soup. I fixed each one of the girls half a sandwich; I divided the can of soup between the four of them. I was so hungry, but I did without. Each time they took a bite I could taste it to. I prayed so hard *for God to give me strength and help me to continue to strive to survive, and keep the faith that he will make the way. My husband never checked on us, helped or showed any compassion for our well being.*

After getting rid of my sorry husband, another problem arose that I couldn't resolve. Daddy came back to live with me. My oldest brother and sisters had moved out on their own. My baby brother and I was the only one home with mama. When she passed the children and I were the only ones living in the house, until daddy came. Daddy never helped out. I guess he thought the bills were going to pay themselves. I did the best I could with the small check I was receiving, and my food stamps.

Times had gotten pretty hard. I couldn't hardly keep the bills paid. I wasn't working at the time, and I was not receiving enough money to pay everything. Daddy knew what was going on but he didn't offer to help. Each weekend he would go visit his girlfriend in Winston-Salem.

One afternoon, as I was coming home, it was so embarrassing, the lights, and water had been turned off. The gas was already off and when I was getting off the bus the Sheriff was sitting our furniture outside. When I got off the bus I walked pass the house until the bus turned the corner. I couldn't hide from the neighbors because they knew I lived there. Soon as the Sheriff would sit something out, daddy would put it back in the house. The neighbors were sitting and standing on the porch watching. I was so embarrassed. We were penniless. I was so tired of suffering, begging, and borrowing. I thought to myself, "It's got to be another way." With no help, I just couldn't do it alone. Daddy moved to Winston-Salem with his girl-friend, and I decided to move in with a friend until things were better. I moved in with Sam. I had been knowing him for years, we were very good friends. After living with Sam for a few months we became more than friends. I was a little happier than before. I didn't have to worry about the bills, my responsibility was my children.

I remember the time when my best friend Rita, wanted me to move in with her. We had been friends ever since we were small. We went to the same school, and we lived in the same neighborhood. Mama use to keep Rita while her mother worked nights. We were like sisters. Rita use to visit most every day. It was on a Monday morning, Sam had gone to work, I could hear the birds singing; it was such a beautiful day. I had

Mama, I Heard Your Cry

just finished cooking breakfast and was getting ready to eat when the doorbell rang. Before I answered it, I heard someone yell, "Matilia, wake up! This is Rita! Open the door!" When she walked in she said, "the food smells good, do you have enough for me?" I said "sure." We both sat down to eat. While eating she confronted me again about moving in with her. I told Rita to give me more time to think about it. I will let her know when I'm ready, if I decide. I had already talked it over with Sam. Three weeks had gone by. I hadn't heard from Rita. A few days later, I received a letter from Social Services giving me two weeks to move out of Sam's apartment. I had no alternative but, to move out. I didn't know where I was going. Daddy had moved. I had no money, it was the middle of the month. I asked myself, "How did they find out?" I called Rita and told her that she would be having guests, my children and "I will be

115

moving in Saturday." She was so excited about me moving in with her. I finally moved in and got settled. I was so glad that was over.

Everything was find in the beginning. As the months went by, Rita started acting differently. I knew that I was paying my part of the bills, we had discussed it before I moved in. I tried to be as fair as possible. It started to bother me. The next day when Rita got home, I asked her, "what was wrong? Was it something I did?" I knew that I didn't do anything wrong. She said, "Why?" In such a nasty tone. I said, "You have been acting strange lately, remember you asked me to move in, I had a place to stay. "She answered, "No Matilia, you didn't do anything wrong. You and your children will have to find somewhere else to live. I need my privacy." I couldn't believe what I was hearing, and I couldn't believe her. I was devastated. I didn't know what to do or say. My children and I had no place to go.

The next day, my children and I left early that morning. I had to find a place for us to live. I didn't know what to do. I couldn't move back with Sam that was impossible. It was drizzling rain when we left that morning. I didn't have an umbrella. While walking with the children, tears filled my eyes because I couldn't help but to think of Mama, I needed her more now than ever. I put in applications all day for an apartment, the children were wore out, poor things. I caught the next bus back to Rita's house. By the time we got there it was pouring down rain, the children and I were soaking wet, and she locked us out. I never owned a key, she never offered me one. I knocked on the door, I rang the bell, no answer. I rang the bell a few more times,

finally her children looked out the window to
see who it was. I yelled, "Open the door! W
are soaked." Cindy, one of Rita's daughters
came to the door and said, "Matilia, we can'
let you in, Mama told us that we better no
open the door for nobody, if we did she wa.
going to beat the hell out of us!" Rita knew
that I lived there, and that her children knew
me. I didn't risk it, I've seen her beat then
many times before. I didn't want them to ge
in trouble. The only thing I knew to do to
protect us was to stand under the little she(
over her porch to keep from getting any
wetter.

The lady next door heard us and let u.
come over until Rita got home. I explained the
situation to her. She shook her head, as she
walked toward the bedroom to find us some
dry clothes. The only thing she said, "you
have to be careful how you treat people

because you will reap what you sow." She made us feel more than welcome, she gave us dry clothes and a hot cup of tea. I was so mad at Rita, I wanted to tell her so badly that Rita was having an affair with her husband, but I change my mind, she was such a friendly person. I couldn't hurt her in any way. I thought to myself, "Lady if you only knew." I thank God today I never mentioned it to her. Rita told me that this neighbor helped her many times. She gave her food when she didn't have any. How could she have such a cold heart toward a person that was so kind to her? Rita was very selfish, she wasn't considerate, and she didn't care about other people's feelings. Rita treated me like a stranger. She didn't allow me to have company at her house. We never got to sleep late on Saturdays. Every Saturday Rita would wake us up early to help her clean the house. Neither of us had a job at the time. I never understood why we had to get up so early. Living with Rita was like being in prison, the only difference was you had more freedom. She believed in having friends. Just about every day Rita had a house full of company, mostly men, and she was talking about having privacy. I was the one that had no privacy. Practically every night Rita was sleeping with a different man. The majority of the time I slept on the hardwood floor. I use to be so uncomfortable. Many times I woke up sore. I use to pray to God asking him to make things better for me and my children. The children shared twin beds and they were comfortable. Her two daughter's shard a bed and my four daughter's shared a bed. Rita use to sell her food stamps to pay her furniture bill. I would buy all the groceries. I use to be so mad. Rita could never help out with groceries.

Mama, I Heard Your Cry

One evening I walked into Rita's house, there were four men sitting at the table eating. I had just bought groceries; I was so angry I grabbed everyone's plate and threw them in the garbage. I didn't mind feeding Rita and her children but, not her company! There was many of days we hardly had enough because she was never chipping in with her stamps. Our food had to last because our children had to eat. I was so fed up with how she had been treating me, one of my best friends I thought. I just couldn't get over it when I needed her the most. I found out when you really need someone they will let you down and strangers will treat you better.

Mama I Heard Your Cry

I Wish I Had

**A father I could have been
proud of to call dad
that's the kind of father I wish
I'd had**

Mama I Heard Your Cry

Chapter 9
My Turning Point

Chapter 9

My Turning Point

*A*fter a few weeks I was lucky enough to find an apartment of my own. I was thrilled! I couldn't wait to move. Mrs. White, who was the owner of the apartment, said that "she would call me when it was ready but that I could come and pick up the key." I couldn't wait to tell Rita. That evening when she get home, I told her that I had my own apartment and that it would be ready in a few days. Rita said, "Why are you moving out?" I said to her, "That's what you wanted, isn't it?" That's what you told me last *week. I thought it was best, at least you will have your privacy. I asked her, "if it was alright if I could continue living with her until my apartment was ready?" She said, "Sure Matilia, you know that I don't mind, I was upset; I didn't mean to be rude." I said, "No hard feelings." I needed a place of my own. I have already promised myself as long as I have health and strength, I'll never live with anyone else. As I sat down, I thought about the time I lived with Rita's mother, and how she treated my children and I.*

I remember when she would beat me with a belt, Rita and the rest of her sisters included, to get us up in the mornings. I'll never forget the time she invited us to Christmas dinner, and when the children and I got there, she had locked all the food in the trunk of her car so we couldn't get any. That was the worse Christmas I ever had. Luckily,

Mama, I Heard Your Cry

Kentucky Fried Chicken was open. That's where we ate Christmas dinner. It brought back memories when I lived with Rita's mother, and how bad she use to treat us. We weren't allowed to cook, and we were not allowed to eat. She had locks on everything. I cannot remember one time that we all sat at her table and ate dinner, not once. And as long as I lived with her, I never felt welcome in her house. I never felt comfortable, and I never felt a part of the family. We were treated so cold. How could we feel a part of anything? I never forgot the time she fed my two youngest daughters one big jar of baby food. All the bad memories began to come back. No matter what, you will never forget it.

There was another time when Rita's mother would take my whole check, and all my food stamps each month when I was

Mama, I Heard Your Cry

living with her. My waiting was in vain each month because she took everything I had. She only paid $33.00 a month; that was for her rent, lights and whatever else she paid. She wouldn't give me money to buy my babies pampers, I was just living there. God is my witness, this is the truth and nothing but the truth. Many times, Rita and I would go out to clubs to meet guys and hope that they would offer us out to eat later that night. We did this often, and most of the time men would buy us what we wanted. We use to be hungry going without eating all day. The next month, I kept $50.00 of my check and $50 of my food stamps. I was determined that she was not going to get all my money that month. When she got home I gave her what I had left. She use to count every penny. When she finished she asked me, "what happened to the rest?" I told her that I spent it, "Oh! She raised hell, she cursed me out, then told me to get the hell out of her house!" It hurt me so bad. I packed my little bit of clothes, and my children and I left walking. I cried, and I cried. I kept thinking about my Mama, wishing that she was alive. A neighbor saw us walking and picked us up, then took us over to my Cousin Pam's house. I lived with her until I could do better. This is the reason why I thought Rita would be different, but she was worse.

Before I left, I told Rita in a nice way how I really felt. I wanted to leave on good terms. Rita was in the kitchen washing dishes, I asked her to sit down for a moment because I wanted to talk with her. I said to Rita, "We have been friends for many years, times have been hard for the both of us trying to raise our children as single parents. And many times we have looked out for one another; when I really needed you, you shut me and my children out. But I'm not mad at you though it hurt. We have been knowing each other too long. I appreciated your friendship. I thought you felt the same about me. In a way, I'm glad that I had the chance to find out the truth for myself, otherwise I wouldn't have known. Everything happens for a reason, and God wanted me to know the truth. My Mama always told me, treat people the way you want to be treated, you never know who you have to rely on in the future. The last thing I told Rita before I left was, who knows, one day you may have to live with me."

Two months passed since I heard from Rita. I had already moved in my apartment. I felt free as a bird, and most of all I was happy again. Another month had passed, still I had not heard from Rita. The next day when I got home, before I could get the key out of the door, the phone rang, guess who? Rita.

When I answered the phone, she asked, "how have you been? What have you been doing with your life?" Have you gotten married? said, to "who?" We laughed, and started conversation. I told her that I was doing great, and how had she been?

Rita said that things had not been working out for her, and that she was sorry about the way everything happened. She said, "Matilia, I know how you felt." I said to her, "don't worry about it." What happened then we cannot change it now. The past is in the past, let's leave it there, we have to go on with our lives and hope for the best. Rita said "Matilia, can I ask you a question without you getting angry?" I said, "sure." I was shocked when she asked me, "if she could move in with me." I didn't know what to say, but I couldn't say no. I asked Rita, "What happened to your apartment?" She said that, "she was evicted," because she couldn't keep up the payments after I moved out. I couldn't turn her down, my heart wouldn't let me. The next week she was prepared to move in. I wanted her to feel welcome in every way. When my friend Sam came over to bring me the money to help out with my rent, I told him what I had planned to do. He yelled, "hell no!" "Are you crazy!" The way she treated you, "how can you ever speak to her again?" I'm saying, "no!" As long as I'm helping you pay rent, it will never happen. After a while the phone rang. It was Rita, she sounded so happy. She said, "Hi, Matilia, don't forget I am moving in tomorrow." I said, "Rita, we have to talk." She asked, "Is something wrong?" I told her that I didn't think that it was a good idea moving in with me. She said, "why did you changed your mind, you thought about the time you lived with me." Yes, I did think about the time I lived with you, but that's not the reason. I don't feel like going into details, I'm sorry. Rita said, "ok thanks Matilia, you take care." That's the last time I heard from Rita. Sam and I got back together. He helped in every way. He did the part my husband didn't do.

From that experience, I've found out that the ones you think are your friends are not always a friend. God showed me things I would have never known if I hadn't moved in with Rita. Now, I believe that things do happen for a reason. And, it's no place like your own home.

Biography:
Chocolate Drop

I was born in Mecklenburg County and my home town is Charlotte, NC. I was my mother's next oldest daughter, born August 22, 1946. Mother made sure that I finished high school (Second Ward High School) and graduated in 1964. A year later, I attended Barber School (Modern Barber College) in Winston-Salem, NC. I lived with my uncle Fred until I finished Barber School. I only had to go nine months. This was the limit before you finished. After I finished Barber School and received my Barber's license, I began cutting hair. My second job was at Taylor's Barber Shop on Beatties Ford Road in the shopping center. This was the most sophisticated barber shop in Charlotte at the time. If you worked at Taylor's Barber Shop you were about something. I cut hair for over forty (40) years. I am now retired.

DEDICATIONS

    I thank God for all the years I've lived and yes! I've had hard times and gone through so much. But God saved my life. Thank you God.

my mother was a good woman
she believed strongly in God
she got up early every morning
she worked so hard

she raised seven of us all by herself
she worked seven days a week
she never got any rest
she stayed on her feet

many days she went to work sick
knowing that she wasn't well
she didn't quit
it's a long story to tell

she had a hard life
she started working at the age of sixteen

Mama, I Heard Your Cry

she was a good wife
so many things interfered with her dreams
her mother passed away when she was only
eight years old her aunt raised her
many she thought had no heart, maybe no
soul
her life seemed to have been out of control

i felt sorry for my mother
seeing her struggling going to work
i couldn't see how she made it any further
but I remembered she put God first
my mother was a strong believer
and a great achiever

i was too young to help out
i didn't understand what it was all about
as I grew older I understood
but I realize she did all she could

i remember those times we had no food to eat
i heard her pray Lord lay me down to sleep
i pray the Lord my soul to keep

Mama, I Heard Your Cry

she didn't give up
she knew that God would be there when times
got rough
it was a thin line but we made it through
it was hard times and our friends were few

although the hills were hard to climb
God didn't fail her not one time
mother we appreciate all you have done
you made a believer out of us
one by one.

Mama I Heard Your Cry

mama, I remember when you worked so hard
to keep food on the table,
but you kept the faith
you believed in God, and knew he was able

you did it all, by the power of Jesus Christ
so many times I wanted to wipe the tears
from your eyes
I felt your pain
I felt it over and over again

I didn't understand
what it was all about
when times got rough
you didn't give up, neither in God, did you
doubt

you strained a lot in life
you was a woman of truth
even when things wasn't right
you looked out for more than just you

Mama, I Heard Your Cry

when you was sick and suffered so long
I prayed for it all to be healed
so that you could survive on your own
mama you was never alone
now you are in a better place
those problems you had you no longer have to
face mama I heard you cry, just as it was
yesterday

I Wish I Had A Father

*I wish I had a father that showed me the way
a father that taught me how to pray*

*A father that would tuck me in bed
A father that made sure my prayers were
said*

*A father that would set me on his knee And
tell me all the good things about me*

*A father I could have faith in A father that I
wouldn't be ashamed to take around my
friends*

*A father that showed me more love A father
to let me know I was often thought of*

*A father that taught me right from wrong A
father that I would be happy to see come
home*

*A father that would wear a smile
A father that remembers that I am his child*

Mama, I Heard Your Cry

A father I could have gone to for advice A father that had greater respect and love for his wife

A father who took the time to take me to six flags So that I could think of the future and forget the past

A father I would have been proud of to call dad that's the kind of father I wish I had

Mama, I Heard Your Cry

Made in the USA
Columbia, SC
26 August 2020